W9-CDX-658

Dear Readers,

In this book you will meet Frederick Douglass. He lived years ago when African American people were slaves in this country. As a young slave boy, Frederick's greatest dream was to free himself and his people.

Because Frederick was brave, smart, and caring, he helped to make our country a better place for himself as well as others. He taught us that we must live not only for ourselves, but for others as well.

Your friend,

Garnet Jackson

Frederick Douglass

Freedom Fighter

Written by Garnet Nelson Jackson
Illustrated by Keaf Holliday

 MODERN CURRICULUM PRESS

Program Reviewers

Maureen Besst, Teacher
Orange County Public Schools
Orlando, Florida

Carol Brown, Director of Reading
Coordinator
Freeport Schools
Freeport, New York

Kanani Choy, Principal
Clarendon Alternative School
San Francisco, California

Barbara Jackson-Nash, Deputy Director
Banneker-Douglass Museum
Annapolis, Maryland

Minesa Taylor, Teacher
Mayfair Elementary School
East Cleveland, Ohio

MODERN CURRICULUM PRESS

13900 Prospect Road, Cleveland, Ohio 44136

A Paramount Communications Company

Library of Congress Catalog Card Number: 92-28777
ISBN 0-8136-5229-4 (Reinforced Binding)   ISBN 0-8136-5702-4 (Paperback)

Text Printed on Recycled Paper

As a young boy, Frederick Douglass lived on Captain Anthony's farm. One day, he chased chickens out of the garden. Keeping chickens out of the garden was Frederick's task.

He also had to clean the yard, drive cows to and from the barn, and run errands. And he always did a good job. If he didn't, he'd be punished.

Frederick was a little slave boy on a farm in Maryland. Because of his busy days, he was always hungry. At suppertime, he gobbled cornmeal mush with other children like himself.

At the end of the day, the tired children huddled on a cabin floor. There they fell soundly asleep.

5

Captain Anthony was a slave owner. He owned many people—men, women, and children. He made them work for him without pay.

Captain Anthony and his helpers punished anyone who did not do as he said.

This was slave life. Everyone awoke very early to begin a hard day's work. And at the end of the day they went to sleep only to get up the next day to work again.

There was hardly any fun at all.

Many times children were kept apart
from their parents. So Frederick was very
happy when his mother visited him.

She lived and worked on a farm a mile
away. She would usually come at night
just as he fell asleep.

The last time Frederick saw his mother,
she brought him a heart-shaped cake.
All Frederick knew about his birthday
was that he was born in February. He
chose February 14, Valentine's Day, as
his birthday.

9

Frederick was unhappy with the way slave owners treated African American people. But he never let anyone know. He just worked hard and kept a smile as he made plans for freedom.

Because Frederick was smart and pleasant, he was well liked. When relatives of Captain Anthony needed a servant, eight-year-old Frederick was chosen. He went to live in the city of Baltimore, Maryland. He was treated well there. He had enough to eat and better clothing to wear.

In Baltimore, he learned to read and write.

Slave children were not allowed to attend school. Frederick, however, traded his food for reading lessons from white children who went to school.

He learned to write some letters by watching carpenters who labeled pieces of wood for ships.

He met his friends in the neighborhood and wrote the letters on a board fence. The children told him the names and sounds of the letters. He put the letters together and made words.

He found an old spelling book and kept it in his pocket at all times.

And, as time passed, he learned all of the words.

Frederick grew up. At age twenty, he dressed as a sailor and ran away to New York City. People who lived in New York and most of the North did not own slaves. Frederick had escaped slavery.

Frederick went all around the North speaking about the evils of slavery.

He wrote articles and books to make people all over the world hate slavery.

17

19

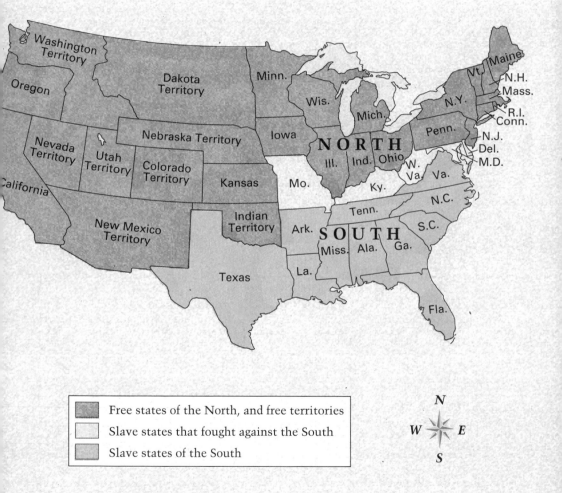

Washington Territory

Oregon

Dakota Territory

Minn.

Wis.

Maine

Vt. N.H.

N.Y. Mass.

Mich. R.I.

Conn.

Nevada Territory

Utah Territory

Nebraska Territory

Iowa

NORTH

Penn.

N.J.

Del.

M.D.

California

Colorado Territory

Kansas

Mo.

Ill. Ind. Ohio W. Va.

Va.

Ky.

New Mexico Territory

Indian Territory

Ark.

SOUTH

Tenn.

N.C.

S.C.

Miss. Ala. Ga.

Texas

La.

Fla.

Free states of the North, and free territories

Slave states that fought against the South

Slave states of the South

N

W E

S

Although many people in America agreed that slavery was wrong, not everyone did. In the South, slave owners did not want African American people to be free.

Northerners and Southerners argued more and more about slavery. At last there was a terrible civil war—the North against the South.

During the war, Frederick met with
President Lincoln. The two men
talked about ways of ending slavery.

Frederick Douglass called on free
African American men to join the
President's army.

Many African American soldiers
fought bravely for the North.

After four years of war, the North
won. Slavery had ended.

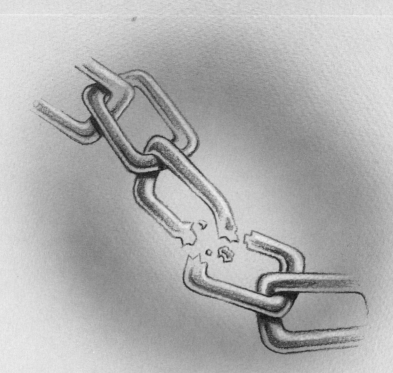

African American people all over the South were joyful to have their freedom. They now had a chance to live and be happy like other people.

Frederick Douglass will always be remembered for helping to bring about this freedom.

Glossary

carpenter (kär´ pən tər) A worker who builds and repairs wooden things, especially the wooden parts of buildings, ships, etc.

civil war (siv´ 'l wôr) War between parts or groups of the same country

errand (er´ ənd) A short trip to do something, often for someone else

freedom (frē´ dəm)   Being free, able to do as one wishes

relative (rel´ ə tiv) A person of the same family, such as a cousin or brother-in-law

slave (slāv) A person who is owned by someone else and has no freedom at all

slavery (slā´ və rē) 1. The practice of owning slaves. 2. The condition of being a slave.

About the Author

Garnet Jackson is an elementary teacher in Flint, Michigan, with a deep concern for developing a positive self-image in young African American students. After an unsuccessful search for materials about famous African Americans written on the level of early readers, Ms. Jackson filled the gap by producing a series of biographies herself. In addition to being a teacher, Ms. Jackson is a poet and a newspaper columnist. She has one son, Damon. She dedicates this book to the memory of her dear mother, Carrie Sherman.

About the Illustrator

Keaf Holliday, a graduate of Cleveland Institute of Art, has worked as a teacher and has been working as a commercial artist for over 10 years. He has illustrated several books, including *Falcon Nest* and *Tales from Africa*, both for children. By combining rich pastel chalks and air brushing, Mr. Holliday creates colors that are soft but firm enough to capture the intensity, drama, and mood of *Frederick Douglass*.